# THE PARENTS' AND PROFESSIONALS' SIMPLE GUIDE TO PDA

*by the same authors*

**The Educator's Experience of Pathological Demand Avoidance**
An Illustrated Guide to Pathological
Demand Avoidance and Learning
*Laura Kerbey*
*Illustrated by Eliza Fricker*
ISBN 978 1 83997 696 4
eISBN 978 1 83997 698 8

**The Teen's Guide to Pathological Demand Avoidance**
*Laura Kerbey*
*Foreword by Dr Julia Woollatt*
*Illustrated by Eliza Fricker*
ISBN 978 1 80501 183 5
eISBN 978 1 80501 184 2

**The Family Experience of PDA**
An Illustrated Guide to Pathological Demand Avoidance
*Eliza Fricker*
ISBN 978 1 78775 677 9
eISBN 978 1 78775 678 6

**Can't Not Won't**
A Story About a Child Who Couldn't Go to School
*Eliza Fricker*
ISBN 978 1 83997 520 2
eISBN 978 1 83997 521 9

**Thumbsucker**
An Illustrated Journey Through an
Undiagnosed Autistic Childhood
*Eliza Fricker*
ISBN 978 1 83997 854 8
eISBN 978 1 83997 855 5

# THE
# PARENTS'
## AND
# PROFESSIONALS'
## SIMPLE GUIDE TO
# PDA

## LAURA KERBEY
## AND ELIZA FRICKER

Illustrated by ELIZA FRICKER

**Jessica Kingsley Publishers**
London and Philadelphia

First published in Great Britain in 2025 by Jessica Kingsley Publishers
An imprint of John Murray Press

Copyright © Laura Kerbey and Eliza Fricker 2025

A CIP catalogue record for this title is available from the British Library
and the Library of Congress

ISBN 978 1 80501 811 7
eISBN 978 1 80501 812 4

Printed and bound in Great Britain by Clays Ltd

Jessica Kingsley Publishers' policy is to use papers that are natural,
renewable and recyclable products and made from wood grown in
sustainable forests. The logging and manufacturing processes are expected
to conform to the environmental regulations of the country of origin.

Jessica Kingsley Publishers
Carmelite House
50 Victoria Embankment
London EC4Y 0DZ

www.jkp.com

John Murray Press
Part of Hodder & Stoughton Ltd
An Hachette Company

The authorised representative in the EEA is Hachette Ireland,
8 Castlecourt Centre, Dublin 15, D15 XTP3, Ireland (email: info@hbgi.ie)

For Mum – for all your help, love and guidance that helped me to become the parent I am today.

For the parents and carers who let their children show them that there was another way. For the parents and carers who were brave enough to go against the grain, and all those who are still finding their way together.

# Acknowledgements

Thank you to all the amazing families that I have had the pleasure of working with over the years. I love working with you and being part of the transformation that can take place in families as your understanding of PDA evolves and grows. Thank you for letting me share your journeys and work with you and your amazing children.

Thank you as always to my friend and illustrator Eliza for making the process of book writing as fun, collaborative and low-demand as possible.

Thank you to everyone at JKP for your continued support.

# CONTENTS

# Introduction

I have been working with neurodivergent children and young people for over 23 years. I started my career as a teacher in the Supported Learning Department of a large mainstream college in the London Borough of Kingston. I think when you teach you get drawn to a certain cohort of students, and I always felt most comfortable teaching the autistic learners.

When the college I worked at asked people to apply for the role of various Champions to support students at the college, I applied for the role of Autism Champion and was delighted when my application was successful. This role gave me an even greater understanding of the autistic students I was working with; however, there were always some students I worked with who didn't seem to quite fit into my understanding of what autism was and wasn't. For these students, my tried and tested approaches, which usually seemed to work pretty well in supporting autistic learners, just did not work. I clearly remember the first time I sat at my desk and googled 'PDA' and had what many parents and professionals describe as 'The Light Bulb Moment' when first reading about it.

When reading about PDA, two things instantly occurred to me.

First, I realised that many of the students I had worked with historically who didn't fit into my understanding of autism were probably PDA.

Second, I realised that my approach with these students had not just been completely wrong, it had also been counterproductive in supporting them. This made me realise that my approach in supporting these learners needed to completely change.

When I left the education system, I set up my own consultancy, and since then I have had the pleasure of working with hundreds of young people with a PDA profile and their families.

As a late-diagnosed neurodivergent adult, I have many special interests, and PDA is certainly one of them. I also confess in my first book, *The Educator's Experience of PDA*, that when you work in education you are not supposed to have favourites, but I do, and they are almost all PDA learners!

This is not a book which is heavy on science, biology or psycho-therapy, but I hope it will be a helpful and positive guide to under-standing PDA that will be beneficial to parents, family members and professionals who work with PDAers. If you are a busy profes-sional who works with a PDAer and you are short on time, then you may just wish to read Chapters 1, 2, 3 and 8.

Finally, I *love* working with PDAers. When they have the right support and feel safe, they are funny, charismatic, kind, loyal and determined. I feel that there is a lot of negativity about PDA, and this is something I am determined to change. I am incredibly posi-tive about PDA, and I hope that reading this book allows you to feel the same.

Chapter 1

# What Is PDA?

> This chapter will be helpful for parents, carers,
> wider family and all professionals to read.

Welcome to *The Parents' and Professionals' Simple Guide to PDA*.
Whether you are reading this book as a parent, a grandparent,
another family member or professional, we hope that you find this
book a helpful, simple and invaluable guide to the complex but
fascinating world of Pathological Demand Avoidance.

PDA is complex and also still, sadly, quite a controversial condition. It is widely thought of as subtype or profile of autism that is
characterised by high anxiety and an overriding need for autonomy.

Autism is assessed by evaluating performance and behaviour in
correspondence with the diagnostic criteria set out by the *Diagnostic and Statistical Manual of Mental Disorders*, 5th edition (DSM-5)
or the *International Classification of Diseases*, Version 11 (ICD-11).

Unfortunately, the way that we assess for autism and other
neurodivergent conditions is still very deficit-based. When assess-
ing for autism, clinicians will assess characteristics and difficulties
associated with:

- social communication and interaction
- restricted and repetitive patterns of behaviour or interests
- sensory differences.

Consideration is also given to the presence of any concerns about a child's early development and the extent to which difficulties cause clinically significant impairment to daily functioning.

Pathological Demand Avoidance (PDA) does not feature in either the DSM-5 or the ICD-11 as a distinct or separate condition. However, PDA is now widely recognised as a profile of development and behaviour within the autism spectrum. The main features of PDA include:

- Resisting and avoiding the ordinary demands of life. Examples of the different types of demands are listed later in this chapter. What is very important to understand about PDA is that demands may be avoided even when the person seems to want to do what has been suggested or asked.
- Using social strategies to avoid demands, such as distracting, giving excuses, flattery, procrastination and negotiation.
- Appearing sociable and having a strong social drive, but lacking depth in their understanding of social and communication skills.
- Excessive mood swings and impulsivity (personally I feel that there is a very big dollop of ADHD in the PDA recipe!).
- The use of role-play and fantasy, sometimes used to an extreme extent to avoid or manage demands.
- 'Obsessive' behaviour that is often focused on other people, resulting in their either loving or loathing them.

Other important features of PDA, which we will explore in this book, include:

- being highly sensitive to non-verbal communication such as tone of voice, facial expressions and body language
- finding praise difficult to tolerate or accept
- preferring spontaneity and novelty to structure and routine
- not recognising status or authority.

You're not the boss of me!

All of the above are essential to be aware of and will be discussed in more detail as we progress through this book.

It would be fair to say that none of us really likes being told what to do. It is a natural response to avoid things which we perceive to be dangerous, uncomfortable, boring, painful, etc. This is known as 'rational' demand avoidance. Being told to do something may make you feel cross, anxious, irritated, etc. For an individual with PDA, being told, asked, or even expected to do something will trigger an immediate feeling of overwhelming anxiety, as demands are perceived as being threats to their autonomy and will make them feel out of control. Just as pollen triggers an uncontrollable reaction in a hayfever sufferer, demands trigger an uncontrollable anxiety-based reaction for PDAers.

## Differences between PDA and more typical autism presentations

Demand avoidance is commonly seen in any autistic profile. Again, just as any of us would, an autistic individual will avoid any situation or environment that causes them to feel unsafe, uncomfortable, etc. We see many children for assessments who will avoid situations that are challenging for them due to the fact that they are autistic. For example, a birthday party is regularly cited by children we assess as being something they find very challenging and that they may try to avoid, but this is often because of the sensory elements such as loud music, unfamiliar and unpredictable food, new people, balloons that pop, etc. Avoiding a birthday party when you are autistic because of these challenges is not 'pathological' demand avoidance, it is actually very rational demand avoidance. Demand avoidance of the pathological kind can appear very irrational at times.

Autistic individuals who are also PDA will present in a specific way – some of these differences may be significant and some may be more subtle.

When parents of children who are autistic and PDA bring them for assessments, they often report that they have been told by other professionals that their child 'does not present as autistic', and they have a very real fear that we will not pick up on their autistic traits (and so not be able to offer an autism with PDA diagnosis). For this reason, I always recommend that, when a child is being assessed for PDA, the assessment team have a thorough understanding and experience of the complexities of the profile.

Some of the differences between PDA and more typical autism presentations include:

- *Social drive*: Often PDAers are very sociable. Many of the children I have worked with over the years have friends but, because they are autistic, don't always fully understand complex social rules of nuances. They may also be bossy and controlling and not understand the impact of this on their friends. In the words of a lovely PDAer I used to work with, 'I am great at making friends but terrible at keeping them.' I have also worked with many children who have found school incredibly difficult but have continued to go because they want to see their friends so much. Of course, all autistic individuals are different, but some of the non-PDA autistic children I have worked with over the years are completely happy in their own company and don't appear to have such a strong social drive as the PDAers I have worked with.

- *Need for routine*: I think this is a really important difference in the profiles. For an individual with PDA, a routine can become a demand, particularly if they have this routine imposed on them. An individual with PDA may like to know what is happening, but they also need autonomy and say in their routine. Knowing that they *have* to do something, but it is time to do it without any autonomy or freedom around it, will cause them anxiety. For a non-PDA autistic individual, *not* having a routine can cause significant anxiety. PDAers will not respond well to the use of traditional autism resources such as 'Now/Next' boards, visual planners, timers, etc., particularly if they have no say in them and they are just presented to them as something that they have to use.

- *Enjoying spontaneity and novelty*: Similarly to the point above, an individual with PDA will likely thrive on the unexpected if it has a high value to them. To give an example of this, a few years ago during a heatwave I was working with two young people. Upon their arrival I gave them the choice of staying in my sweltering office or taking our session to the park with a drink or ice-cream. My PDA client jumped at the chance to do something different, but my autistic non-PDA client told me he wasn't expecting to do that and chose to stay at the office despite the heat, he just could not manage the unexpected change.

- *Hyperempathy/emotions*: One of the biggest myths about autism is that autistic individuals lack empathy, which is absolute rubbish! I think that some of the autistic individuals I have worked with absolutely have empathy, but they sometimes find it hard to express it. PDAers, however, seem hyperempathetic at times, and other people's distress can cause significant distress to them.

- *Rewards and behaviour systems*: Whereas a structured reward or motivating system *may* work for some autistic children, a child with PDA is likely to find this incredibly anxiety-provoking due to the pressure it creates as a demand to be good. Sometimes the 'reward' on offer to the PDAer is just of no value to them; so things like stickers, house points, etc. will not motivate them. PDAers are also very clever and will find all sorts of loopholes in reward systems.

- *Demand avoidance*: Yes, you will see demand avoidance in an autism profile but as I have already explained, this demand avoidance will be to avoid things that the individual finds uncomfortable, challenging, boring, etc. and is therefore rational. An individual with PDA will experience demand avoidance about the things that they want to do as well as the things that they don't want to do due to the anxiety these demands cause, and therefore the demand avoidance can be seen as pathological and not rational. An individual with a PDA profile will go to great lengths to avoid demands, and they may use a range of creative and very clever strategies to avoid things they see as demands. Parents will often say to me, 'If only they spent as much time *doing* the thing they have been asked to do as they spend avoiding it!'

Just as everyone who is autistic is different, everyone with PDA is different too. Although PDAers will share many characteristics, PDA is a spectrum, and everyone with PDA is a unique individual and will therefore need a unique, individual, person-centred approach.

## Taking a low-demand approach with PDAers

As demands trigger anxiety, and therefore demand avoidance, a 'low-demand approach' is often recommended with PDAers.

In order to reduce demands, we need to understand what demands are. There are different types of demands, and demands are absolutely everywhere! Examples of direct demands include:

- Go and clean your teeth.
- Go to bed.

- Get ready.
- Start your work.
- Go and have a wee!

Examples of more subtle demands include:

- It's time for dinner.
- It's bedtime.
- You need to get ready now.
- Let's start this now.

Some demands are silent – we don't even need to open our mouths to create them. These would include non-verbal communications and expectations that are understood without being articulated. For example:

- placing a meal in front of someone, which creates a demand to eat
- placing work in front of someone, which creates an expectation to do it
- tapping or just looking at your watch or a clock
- expecting an individual to say 'please' or 'thank you' (when they may not want what they have been given or be grateful for it!)
- expecting certain behaviours that are considered 'good manners'
- providing a timetable, planner, routine or schedule to be followed.

An individual with PDA will even experience demand avoidance about internal or self-imposed demands. Examples of self-imposed demands may include:

- going to sleep
- eating
- personal hygiene
- speaking
- engaging in hobbies or interests
- toileting.

People with PDA often really want to engage in things, but the demand of doing those things triggers their anxiety, which causes the demand avoidance. Using the example of hayfever again, lots of

CAN'T

*not*

WON'T

people with hayfever love being outdoors and around flowers – but this triggers their allergies, meaning they can't stay there for long.

Remember, PDA is not about not *wanting* to things. PDA is about not being *able* to do things.

We have to remember that, although parenting or supporting an individual with PDA can be challenging and frustrating at times, it is *far* more challenging and frustrating for the person experiencing PDA, particularly if they feel that they are not understood.

Adopting a low-demand approach that is rooted in autonomy, respect, connection, equality, humour and reciprocity can be, and I quote many parents and educational professionals here, 'trans-formative' and life-changing, not just for the individual with PDA, but also for their parents, wider family and the professionals working with them.

Finally, if you are a professional working with a PDAer, then please remember that reasonable adjustments should be based on need and not diagnosis. Some of the best schools I have worked with have done incredible work with children with PDA who don't have a formal diagnosis of a PDA profile.

And, if you are a parent or family member reading this, then please remember that your child does not need a diagnosis of PDA for you to make the changes needed to support your child.

Personally, I feel that a communication style that is rooted in autonomy, respect, connection, autonomy, equality, humour and reciprocity will be beneficial to *any* child or young person.

Chapter 2

# Anxiety of the PDA Kind

> This chapter will be helpful for parents, carers,
> wider family and all professionals to read.

To understand PDA, we have to understand the anxiety that individuals with PDA experience pretty much all of the time. Although we can't always see it, someone with PDA is a hypervigilant, hypersensitive individual who is constantly on alert to the threat of the demands around them.

Neurodiversity and anxiety go hand in hand. I don't think I have ever met a neurodivergent person who does not have a significantly higher baseline of anxiety than the average neurotypical person.

A helpful way to understand the anxiety that neurodivergent people experience is by using the Anxiety Bucket Analogy.

All of us carry around an invisible anxiety bucket all day, and throughout the day our bucket is being filled with things that make us feel stressed, anxious, angry or uncomfortable. For a neurotypical individual, their bucket has lots of holes in it, so what goes into the bucket quickly gets processed and can trickle out of the bucket. This means that for a neurotypical individual it takes something big or unusual for their bucket to fill up.

The neurodivergent individual's bucket is different as it does not have any holes or maybe has one or two tiny pinprick holes. This means that every time a neurodivergent individual experiences something that makes them feel stressed, anxious, angry or uncomfortable their bucket will keep filling up as there is nowhere for the stuff pouring in to go. What is essential to remember about PDA, is that demands will fill the bucket up as they cause uncontrollable anxiety to the individual with PDA.

Another difference in the buckets is that the PDAer's bucket is almost never completely empty, so their capacity for demands and other things that fill the bucket is already reduced. This means that their buckets will appear to fill up more quickly than other people's.

When a PDAer has low anxiety, their tolerance to demands will increase, this is because their bucket still has capacity for further demands. On the other hand, when the PDAer has high anxiety, their bucket has no capacity left so their tolerance to demands will decrease.

**Low Anxiety + High Autonomy = High Demand Tolerance**

**High Anxiety + Low Autonomy = Low Demand Tolerance**

It is important to remember that the more anxious an individual feels, the less cognitively able they will become. As our anxiety rises, our brains will go into a 'survival' mode and will therefore be far less capable of processing, thinking clearly, etc. It is also common for us not to be able to form memories when we are very anxious.

LOWER

DEMAND

ANXIETY

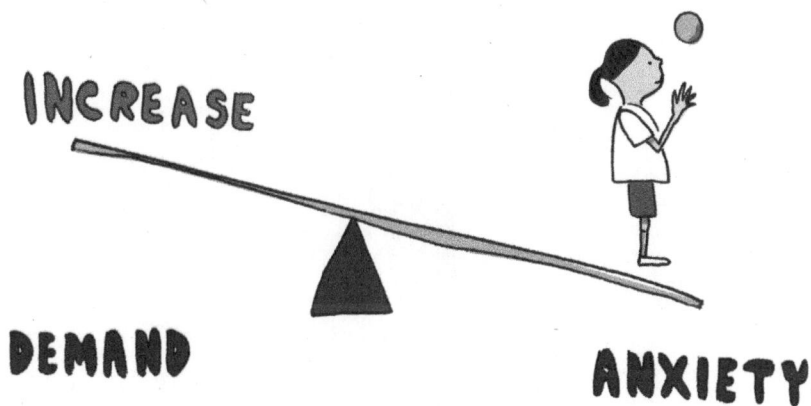

INCREASE

DEMAND

ANXIETY

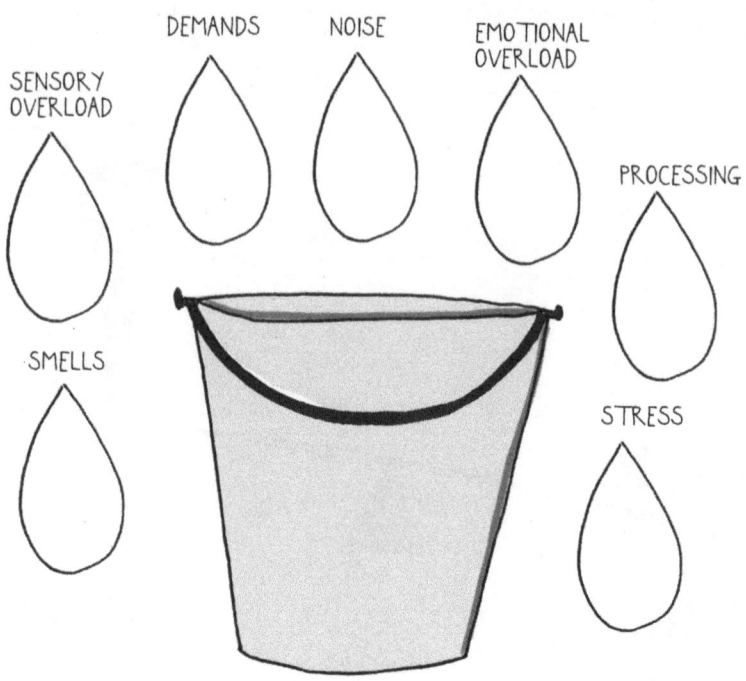

Once the bucket is filled up, the individual with PDA will experience an uncontrollable anxiety-based response, such as fight, flight, freeze, etc. This will be covered more in Chapter 6.

## Filling and emptying the PDA bucket

One of the most helpful ways you can support a PDAer is by knowing the answers to two questions:

- What fills their bucket up?
- What empties their bucket?

If you can reduce the bucket fillers and increase the number of holes in the bucket, you can help to prevent the bucket from overflowing. I have found that discussing this with the individual with PDA has been really beneficial, especially if they are able to do this themselves. If they recognise what is happening and what they need to do to avoid overwhelm, they can begin to self-advocate.

The rate at which the bucket fills up will vary from individual to individual and also day by day. When I worked in my school I would often see a pattern whereby a child would have a really 'good' day and seem able to tolerate many demands, and I would think, 'Yes! We have cracked it!' Then the following day the child would either be unable to come in or would come to school but not be able to cope with any demands as the bucket would still be full from the previous day.

Some of the children I work with who are in schools will arrive at school with a very full bucket due to the huge number of demands that they have had to deal with just to get there.

We have to understand that one demand could be made up of many 'micro demands' that are all causing the bucket to gradually fill. For example, the demand to 'get ready for school now' is actually more like 20 micro demands such as:

- wake up
- get out of bed
- go to the toilet
- eat breakfast
- clean teeth
- get dressed
- get shoes on
- put a coat on
- remember bag
- get in the car, etc.

## Understanding masking

PDAers are extremely proficient maskers, which means it is extremely common for children and young people with PDA to appear 'fine' in school, when in reality their bucket is slowly filling up all day. The PDAer may don the mask of 'the well-behaved child' and will avoid asking for help, or even accepting help. Sometimes children will present very differently with grandparents or at friends' houses, so it can be hard for all family members to understand the challenges that parents are dealing with every day.

This means that the child or young person ends their school or college day with a completely full bucket, so when the child is released from school or returns home from their grandparents or friend's house back into the care of their safe person or place, the bucket is so full it bursts.

Another analogy used to explain this is the Coke Bottle Effect. Just as a bottle of Coke (or other soft drink) that is being shaken all day will explode when opened, the child or young person with PDA will explode or implode at the end of the day (i.e. will experience meltdown or shutdown). Meltdowns are usually fairly obvious to the people around the person experiencing them, but shutdowns may be less obvious as the person experiencing them may internalise all their anxiety, become non-verbal, or just feel the need to hide away or sleep. Shutdowns are a way of minimising input when the person cannot tolerate any more. Meltdowns and shutdowns are equally difficult for the person experiencing them.

If you are an educational professional reading this, then I have a very important request. If you have a parent who comes to you and tells you that their child is really struggling with school, please, please, please, even if you don't see that the child appears to have *any* difficulties during their time with you, don't tell that parent that their child 'seems fine in school'. This can be very disheartening to hear. Instead, you need the parent to feel heard, and work with them to suggest how their child's individual needs could be supported. Many PDA strategies, like regular check-ins, movement breaks, a safe person and a safe space, can be incorporated into a child's day, and then regular communication with parents can establish if these have had a positive impact at home too.

It is very common when we are doing assessments for the information that is provided by schools to look completely different to the information that parents present to us. This is not because the parents are lying or exaggerating or because the school isn't being diligent – it is often because the PDAer is such a proficient masker that often schools and colleges just don't see the same challenges or behaviours.

There is now significant research into the links between long-term masking and mental illness, so it is essential that schools

and colleges understand that just because a child or young person 'looks fine' it does not mean that they are.

Anxiety may take many guises, and it is essential to realise that not all anxious people *look* anxious. Anxiety may look like anger, shyness, excitement, overconfidence or even arrogance. Some children and young people may laugh when they are anxious, which can make other people feel that they are not taking situations seriously. Some of the most anxious individuals I have worked with do not look anxious at all, which has been confusing for parents and professionals when it comes to supporting their needs.

ANXIETY...

## Understanding hypersensitivity

Because they are so anxious, PDAers are hypervigilant and highly sensitive to their environment, and this includes the people in it. When I run parents' workshops I regularly ask, 'Put your hand up if your child has ever accused you of shouting when you weren't,' and pretty much *every* hand goes up. I also ask, 'Put your hand up if your child has ever accused you of being angry with them when you weren't,' and again almost every hand goes up.

PDAers are hypersensitive because they are so hypervigilant. A good way to describe this is to think of a smoke detector in your home. A neurotypical person is like a smoke detector that goes off if there is smoke or fire in your home, which is the correct level of sensitivity. Now imagine a smoke detector that goes off if someone walks past your house smoking a cigarette, this is like a PDAer. This smoke detector is triggered by tiny amounts of smoke, the way a PDAer is hypersensitive and triggered by any demands or other threats in their environment that make them feel that they are losing autonomy or control.

## Autonomy and control

There is an important relationship between anxiety and control that all of us will experience. For many of us, anxiety will be triggered when we feel we have no control, and this is very much the case for a PDAer, as the less control and autonomy they feel they have, the more anxious they will be. Conversely, the more autonomy and control a PDAer has, the less anxious they will be.

As already mentioned, autonomy is of vital importance to an individual with PDA. People often describe PDA as an 'an anxiety-driven need for control'. But I, and many others, feel that autonomy is of even more importance to a PDAer.

PDA has been renamed by several advocates as a 'Pervasive Drive for Autonomy' (Tomlin Wilding) or a 'Persistent Drive for Autonomy' (Dr Wenn Lawson). Personally, I prefer these to 'Pathological Demand Avoidance' as they are not only more positive but they explain more about why demands are avoided.

When someone with PDA has autonomy, they feel that they are in control and therefore have less of a need to control others. When PDAers don't have autonomy, then this is when you are more likely to see controlling behaviours.

A good way to understand this is by thinking about the following scenario: Imagine you are driving a car, and in the seat next to you your 'helpful' passenger starts saying things like, 'Oh – there's a cyclist ahead, better slow down,' or 'Careful, you're going 31mph when it's a 30 zone,' or 'The lights ahead are going red now!' At first you would likely feel a bit irritated or annoyed, then if they continued with their helpful advice you would probably start to feel angry. You may feel that your skills as a driver are being questioned, and this may make you feel patronised and undermined.

Now imagine that your 'helpful' passenger starts trying to grab the wheel of the car and actually change the direction you are driving in. This is likely to make you feel very unsafe, and you would probably stop the car and tell them to get out! If you saw that person walking down the street in the future you would be unlikely to offer them a lift.

Now, sometimes, having a passenger is a good thing, but you need your passenger to be genuinely helpful. You may ask for directions, or for them to pass you something. You may need directions if you are unsure of the route, and they may suggest a quicker route if there are roadworks of delays. You may just appreciate their company on boring drives.

This is a good way to illustrate the best way to support someone with PDA. In this scenario, you are the passenger. PDAers need autonomy to feel safe, and being autonomous means being self-driven. Taking away their autonomy will make the PDAer feel unsafe, and they will feel the need to get control back. You need to be the genuinely helpful passenger who is there to support and enhance the journey, not to take over the steering and make the driver feel unsafe.

As already stated, there is an important link between the anxiety a PDAer feels and their tolerance of demands. While it makes sense to try and reduce the anxiety that PDAers feel, we have to be incredibly careful when advising PDAers of how to manage their anxiety, because telling them what to do is in itself going to create a demand. Telling someone with PDA to 'take a nice deep breath' is not going to help them! Instead, it can be better to role-model how you feel when you are anxious yourself. For example, you could say, 'When I am anxious, I feel panicky inside and I can't focus properly. I have to stop and take some deep breaths to calm myself down. I try to take five breaths, counting in for five and out for five each time.' Or you could say, 'I felt so angry today when someone stole my parking space, but I managed to count backwards from ten and stopped myself from shouting at him and calling him a very rude name!'

It may be helpful to discuss your child's anxiety using the Anxiety Bucket Analogy at a time when they feel calm, and also to teach them about the function of their anxiety, too, so that they know it is OK to feel anxious, that anxiety is actually a way for us to sense danger and keep safe and not a bad emotion.

## Strategies for managing anxiety

Another very helpful approach that I have used when supporting PDAers with their anxiety is to use scaling. Scales can help individuals identify when they are feeling unsafe or uncomfortable without actually having to name the emotion that they are feeling. A book called *The Incredible 5-Point Scale* by Kari Dunn Buron and Mitzi Curtis is extremely helpful for advising on how to create scales for all sorts of things (see 'Resources' section at the end of this book).

I have found that using a three-point scale is the easiest and most effective way to use a scale. For example:

1.= I feel OK.

2 = This is getting tricky but I can give it a go.

3 = This is too hard. I need to leave now.

If your child knows that they can tell you that they are on a '3' when they are out or in a situation that makes them feel unsafe or uncomfortable, then this in itself can help reduce their anxiety as they know they have an escape route. If doing this, it is really important to honour a request to leave, so the child learns to trust the scale.

You can also use scales to help identify the intensity of emotions:

1 = I feel calm.

2 = I am getting angry.

3 = I feel really mad now.

I would also advise you use this language yourself around your PDAer to role-model its effectiveness rather than telling them to use it, which will create a demand.

You may seek a therapist to support your child with their anxiety, but it would be essential to ensure that any therapist who works

| 1 | I feel OK. |
| 2 | This is getting tricky but I can give it a go. |
| 3 | This is too hard, I need to leave now. |

with your child either has understanding and experience of PDA or is willing to learn about it. I am often asked by parents, 'What is the best therapy for a child with PDA?' My answer to this is that it is not the therapy but the therapist that is important. If your child has a good connection and feels safe with the therapist, then this is the crucial foundation for them to work together. The children and young people with PDA that I work with access all sorts of therapy, such as art, music, animal, etc. Many don't have formal therapy but instead have safe relationships with sports coaches, riding instructors or tutors. I also recommend mentoring with safe people that the PDAer can relate to.

I am also asked regularly about medication for children and young people with PDA. I don't feel that medication should ever be the first point of call for a young person; however, I have seen medication work absolute wonders too, particularly for teenagers who are experiencing high anxiety and low mood. Medication should always be discussed with a medical professional and should always be something that your child feels that they have control and autonomy over too.

Chapter 3

# How to Support a PDAer

This chapter will be helpful for parents, carers,
wider family and all professionals to read.

One of the most important parts of parenting is caring or supporting a child so they feel safe. One of my favourite expressions is 'The
antidote to anxiety is trust'.

Connections and trust are everything to PDAers and the more
connections they have with people, the safer they will feel.

Taking a genuine interest in a PDAer's interests is a fantastic
way to connect with them. Even if their special interest is not something you would want to do, just sitting and talking to them about
the things they love will help them feel connected to you. This is
something that all family members and family friends can do and
is such an important part of maintaining a genuine connection
and building good relationships.

PDAers are autistic, so they probably will not enjoy or see the
point of small talk, but 'Big Talk' about the things that they love

# connection
## AND
## TRUST

# BIG TALK

I bought a really nice plant this morning, it's like the one in my living room but this one has white flowers in the springtime.

*not*

# SMALL TALK

Hi. How are you?

and are interested in is far more valuable to them. Big Talk has a purpose and is also a brilliant way to build connection and trust.

Perhaps you could ask the PDAer in your life why they love Minecraft, Anime, etc. so much? They may enjoy sharing facts or teaching you about the thing that they love doing. They may also be very protective about it and not want to share, and that's OK too. Just sitting and sharing space together without placing demands on a PDAer can be really valuable time to spend together.

# Using rewards and natural consequences

If you are a parent reading this, you have probably realised already that traditional reward systems like sticker charts, time out and the naughty step do not work for PDAers. (I know a parent who literally spent a whole day taking her son back to the naughty step as she was told he had to sit there for a minute for every year of his age. This child was four years old, and every time the timer got to almost four minutes he would look at his mum and get up!)

Reward systems don't work for PDAers because they make them feel out of control and can actually increase their anxiety. Unless the child or young person sees the value of the demand it will seem meaningless to them.

Conversely, some rewards will seem too big and important. Dangling something that a PDAer really wants in front of them and telling them that they can have it if they are 'good' or compliant with a demand will likely cause them even more anxiety. They will be so worried that they may not get the thing that they want, they may even sabotage getting the item – at least then they are in control, even if it means losing the item they were coveting.

Rewards for PDAers need to be of value and they need to be instantaneous too. Parents are sometimes embarrassed to tell me that 'bribery' works for their child, but I then ask them if they would go to work if they did not get paid!

'Natural consequences' are often really important for PDAers to work out themselves. For example, telling your child that they 'need to go to bed' when they don't feel tired will not result in your child willingly and happily snuggling down and turning the light off. *But*, if your child sees the value in going to bed early, for example because the next day they want to be awake early to make sure they get the update for a new online game, then it is more likely they will go to bed. (Or they may just decide to pull an all-nighter instead!)

A child who doesn't put their coat on when they go to the park may realise that being cold prevented them from enjoying their trip, and next time may take their coat without you suggesting it.

It can be helpful for *you* to talk about natural consequences too. Instead of saying, 'Go and have a shower and then you can go on the Xbox,' you could say, 'It's great you had a shower. I am sure you will feel more comfortable, and you have time to play on your Xbox now.'

## Praise

Natural consequences can also be a more appropriate way to 'praise' a PDAer. Having difficulties with praise is something that we look at as part of the assessment process and is seen as a feature of the presentation. *Not* praising someone with PDA is something that can feel very alien to both parents and professionals, and it was certainly one of the things I had to consciously think about when I first started working with PDAers.

Praise can be very difficult for PDAers to accept, and this is due to a variety of reasons:

- Praise can set up an expectation to repeat or improve an action or behaviour (and remember, expectations are a kind of demand).
- Praise may feel patronising, as the PDAer feels that they are equal to you.
- Praise may feel disingenuous. As one boy I assessed recently told me, 'I can only accept praise if I feel that I deserve it.'

## Shielding our children

If you are reading this as a parent, you will probably be working really hard to create a safe, low-demand environment for your child at home; but if people come into this environment who don't understand the approach you are taking, this will make the environment unsafe for your child. Your role as a parent is to try to shield them from the demands that visitors, even well-meaning ones, can put on your child. If you are reading this as a family member or friend, it is important to understand that parents of PDAers are probably doing things very differently to the way you did things or are doing things, but they are doing what is right for their child, not doing things wrong.

Speak to your family and friends (or just give them this book) and help them understand that your child's home is their safe place. Just having a family member or friend in the home creates all sorts of additional demands for your child such as:

- saying hello and goodbye
- being polite
- behaving!

- having to answer questions such as 'How are you getting on at school/college?' etc.
- eating with unfamiliar people at a table.

Give granny a big kiss.

Having visitors and guests in your home will make your child more anxious, which means that the additional demands we place on them will feel even harder. Our own expectations of 'Please be good!' will also be picked up on by your child as they are so super-sensitive to other people's emotions.

This is why special occasions such as birthdays and Christmas can be so challenging for PDAers. These family events, which are supposed to be fun and happy occasions, are absolutely loaded with demands and often result in lots of tears and frustration (from both parents and children alike!). I remember speaking to a parent once in early January who told me how awful her Christmas had been, saying, 'I just wanted to have one nice day!'

For someone with PDA, just knowing that the people around you want to have a 'nice day' will create demands and expectations and will probably result in the day being anything but 'nice'.

It is really important that we shield our children from the additional demands and ensure that they maintain as much autonomy as possible on these occasions. Allowing them to still have access to their safe space, safe foods, etc. is also really important. You may find that your child is more willing to engage in 'special' occasions when they feel that they have autonomy to leave, pop in and out, etc. You should never force your child to be involved.

After high-demand situations, such as family events, special occasions, trips out or school, the individual with PDA is likely to have a very full bucket. It is essential to give them time and space to let the bucket empty, so factor this in when planning events and activities and ensure you lower demands after such activities. For example, if your child is in school, don't ask them lots of questions when you pick them up and allow them to go to their quiet space (probably their room) and engage in low-demand activities before you place more demands on them to do things like get changed, do homework, sit with the family for dinner, etc.

## Curbing your enthusiasm

When parenting, caring or supporting individuals with PDA, it is essential to know when to curb your enthusiasm – especially if you start to see something going well. I understand that this is a tricky balance to find, but if an individual with PDA wants to do something, particularly if they have previously been unable to engage in very much, then it can be hard not to get too excited. However, your excitement will add to the pressure to do 'the thing' (whatever it is), which means that they may not be able to do it anymore. In this situation I would step back, simply try and facilitate the event happening, involve the individual with PDA as much as possible and have a back-up plan (or two) in case their anxiety means that they cannot follow through with what they wanted to do.

## Choosing language carefully

The language we use around individuals with PDA is really important. As mentioned in Chapter 1, demands are everywhere, and our language is often very demand-laden, offering the PDAer very little autonomy.

Using choices, challenges and declarative language (i.e. comments or statements) can ensure that the individual with PDA feels that they have more autonomy. This will soften the impact of any demands.

As a reminder, here are some of the demands identified in Chapter 1.

Direct demands:

- Go and clean your teeth.
- Go to bed.
- Get ready.
- Start your work.
- Go and have a wee!

Here are some suggestions for more appropriate ways to present these to someone with PDA:

- *I wonder if you could brush your teeth standing on one leg?*
- *Would you like to read to yourself or me to read to you before you go to bed?*
- *I'm ready to go, would you like me to tell you when it's time to leave?*
- *Would you like to start with this piece of work or this piece of work?*
- *I am going to go for a wee before we leave so we don't have to stop on the way.*

Subtle demands:

- It's time for dinner.
- It's bedtime.
- You need to get ready now.
- Let's start this now.

Here are some suggestions for more appropriate ways to present these to someone with PDA:

- *Would you like to come down for dinner or eat in your room?*
- *Would you like me to come and say goodnight in 10 minutes or 20 minutes?*
- *Can you get ready on your own or would you like some help?*
- *I am just doing X, if you let me know when you are ready we can start.*

I would like to offer a word of caution here though. PDAers are usually *very* clever and may work out that you are using 'strategies' to get them to comply with demands. I know parents who have attended PDA workshops, and their child has turned around and said, 'You are doing things differently now!' and education staff who have feigned interest in topics as a way of getting a child to complete work. You risk damaging your relationship with someone with PDA if you use any sneaky strategies to trick them into compliance. PDAers need authenticity and will sniff out anything that is fake and any deliberately hidden demands straight away. To put it bluntly, PDAers have the best BS detectors of anyone you are likely to meet!

A second word of caution here. You will see that I have used examples of choices in the possible alternatives above. Choices *can* be very helpful for PDAers because it gives them more autonomy, but making a choice can still be a demand, and if someone is feeling very anxious then making a decision can be really hard as they may feel frozen. Also, if neither choice is appealing, then neither is going to be chosen! I don't eat meat, so if someone offers me a ham sandwich or a roast beef sandwich, I am not going to choose either! But, if I am hungry I may accept the offer of some toast and butter even though this would not be my first choice for a snack.

Sharing demands with your PDAer can also be extremely beneficial. First, if you share a demand and do it together you make it smaller; and second, sharing demands makes them feel more reciprocal, which can really help to improve connection and relationships. Remember that your PDAer feels like your equal, so it will feel very unfair to them if you ask them to do things that you would not be willing to do yourself. Plus, of course, doing things together means that they will get done much quicker!

As an example, rather than saying to a PDAer 'Tidy your room,' you could suggest tidying their room together and also pointing out the benefits or having a tidy room: 'You will have more space for your gaming stuff if we tidy your room.' You can also make the demand of tidying fun by playing music, etc., too.

There will, of course, be times when your PDAer cannot manage the demands, even when you have adapted your language. Although this can be disappointing and frustrating, it is really important that your disappointment does not create additional pressure for the child. If, for example, you pay for your child to join a club and then they cannot attend, avoid saying, 'Oh another thing I have paid for that you can't finish!' Remember that they are hypersensitive to your emotions, and they will soak these up like a sponge, so your feelings will make their anxiety worse. The PDAer is likely to be feeling just as disappointed and frustrated as you are, and empathising with this will be really important. Saying something like, 'I am sorry we didn't get to do X today. I know you were looking forward to it earlier. I am disappointed too but don't worry we can try again another day,' may help to reduce the negative emotions the PDAer is experiencing, and it is OK to let them know how you feel about it too.

As I mentioned earlier, demands don't always have to be spoken out loud. Here are the examples of silent demands we looked at earlier with some more PDA-friendly suggestions.

Silent demands:

- placing a meal in front of someone, which creates a demand to eat

- placing work in front of someone, which creates an expectation to do it
- tapping or just looking at your watch or a clock
- expecting an individual to say 'please' or 'thank you' (when they may not want what they have been given or be grateful for it!).

PDA-friendly suggestions:

- *Saying 'Dinner is on the table if you are hungry.'*
- *Offering a few choices of work for someone to look at.*
- *Not tapping your watch!*
- *Not worrying about manners!!*

You can see that for the third and fourth of these examples I have decided to drop the demand entirely. This is because sometimes when we are supporting PDAers we need to pick our battles, and we will look at this more in the next chapter.

Chapter 4

# Doing Things Differently

This chapter will be helpful for parents, carers, wider
family members and friends, and professionals
such as social workers, SENCOs, education welfare
officers or home school link workers to read.

If you are reading this as a parent, then you probably now realise that a 'traditional' parenting approach is not going to work with your PDA child.

If you are reading this as a grandparent, family member or friend then you probably realise that the way that you parented your children is not going to be the same way your children need to parent theirs.

And if you are reading this as a professional, then you will need to teach, support or treat a child or young person with PDA very differently to the ways you have treated other children and young people before too.

As parents, we tend to either do things the same way that our parents did or realise that the way we were parented is definitely not the way that we want to parent ourselves. Either way we are being influenced by the way we were brought up.

As parents, we are bombarded with messages of how we *should* parent. We are influenced by TV shows, adverts, our families, friends and the invisible 'they' who tell us what the perfect parent looks like. We also receive unwelcome advice about our parenting style, and it can be hard to do things differently from what we think 'they' think we should be doing or what seems to be in the invisible book of what constitutes a 'good parent'.

But guess what? Your PDA child has not read and has absolutely no intention of reading the rule book, so parenting and caring for a child with PDA means throwing the rule book out the window!

## How a PDAer understands hierarchy

An important factor to consider when parenting a child with PDA is that they are unlikely to see hierarchy. They will not do what you ask, tell or expect them to do just because you are the parent, grandparent or adult. I have always described PDAers as being 'adults trapped in children's bodies', and because of this, many children with PDA will engage in equalising behaviour because they see themselves as your equal.

This means that a 'do as I say not as I do' approach will absolutely not work with PDAers.

Many neurotypical children will do what they have been asked to do by adults without questioning it, but this is unlikely to happen with PDAers; first, because they see themselves as equal to adults, and second, because they need to have factual reasons explaining why demands are important. Without reasons, demands will seem pointless and arbitrary, so it is important to depersonalise the demand and explain the reasons behind them. It can also be helpful to show empathy around the fact that some things have to be done, for example by saying 'I know you find wearing a seatbelt uncomfortable, but it is against the law not to wear it. If the police see that we are not wearing our seatbelts they will pull me over and I may get a fine or points on my licence.' Simply saying 'because I said so' is not going to wash with a PDAer!

That's poisonous.

It's twice a day.

Seatbelts have to be worn.

Only when the light is green.

# FACTS
## NOT
### Opinions

Parenting and caring for a child with PDA means doing things that are best for you and your child. It can feel very strange when you start to deviate from the path you thought you were going to take as a parent, but I honestly don't know a parent who has regretted implementing a low-demand PDA-friendly approach, even though it may have felt like it went against everything they thought they would do.

## Choosing your battles

An important question you need to ask yourself when you are parenting or supporting individuals with PDA is 'Does it really matter?'

Several years ago, I was working with a lovely family. They had one neurotypical child and then a younger child who was referred to me for support with his anxiety. Although he was 'well behaved' at school, his behaviour at home challenged his parents, and this was clearly causing a lot of tension between his mum and dad who had very opposing views on the best way to parent their son. The boy's mum had been on one of my parenting workshops and was seeing the positive impact of implementing a low-demand approach, but her husband was finding it much harder to do and would say that his wife was being 'too soft' and letting their son 'get away' with things. I agreed to see the boy's dad on his own for some sessions. At our first session I could tell that he was going to find changing the way he parented a challenge, but he did seem open to trying. One of the many issues that we discussed in that conversation was how difficult the mornings were and how frustrating this parent was finding it all.

The following week the dad arrived for his session and the first thing he said to me was, 'Laura, I have done something this morning that I have never done before and I need you to tell me that I did the right thing!' He looked like he was going to confess something terrible to me, so I tentatively asked what had happened and he said, 'I let Tommy watch his iPad at the breakfast table this morning!'

'And...?' I asked.

'He ate his breakfast, got ready without any issues, and for the first time in ages we left for school on time and he seemed really happy!'

He went on to explain that there had been no shouting that morning and minimal stress, and yet despite recognising how much easier the morning had been, this dad was left with a feeling of unease that he had done something 'wrong'.

Of course, I reassured this lovely dad that he had done nothing wrong at all. It just felt wrong as it was so different to the way that he had been doing things, even though the results of this had caused so much stress and anxiety all round.

## Changing expectations

As well as asking 'Does it really matter?' We also need to question 'Who does it matter to?'

When we are parenting, we often ask or expect our children to do certain things because it matters to us, but if an individual with PDA does not see the point, value or the 'what's in it for me' factor, they are going to see the demand as either too big to manage or not worth the anxiety that complying may cause. The expenditure to comply will just be too big for too little payback.

Things that may matter more to parents than they do to the child with PDA might include things like:

- manners
- personal hygiene
- going to bed at bedtime
- sitting together to have a family meal
- having a 'nice' day out
- behaving in a certain way in certain places
- ...and lots, lots more!

Parenting a child with PDA means that we have to view activities and events through their eyes. As parents, what we see as going out for a 'nice meal' in a restaurant is likely viewed as an intolerable event for a child with PDA due to all the demands that this will create. Just the expectation of enjoying a meal out means there's a risk that everyone is going to be disappointed! We have to manage the expectations we place on our children with PDA very differently and ask ourselves if we have set them too high.

Celebrations such as Christmas and birthdays can cause enormous anxiety for PDAers because of the demands that they create. It can be hard for us as parents to change our own expectations around these events, but it is very likely that you will have to adapt these occasions to reduce demands to lessen the anxiety that your children is experiencing. For example, telling your child what their presents are in advance, not wrapping presents, not expecting your child to eat a traditional Christmas dinner or sit and watch everyone open their presents could spell the difference between a 'good day' and an awful day for you and for them.

Whilst managing your own expectations, you will probably need to manage the expectations of wider family. Explaining PDA to others will hopefully help them understand why you are doing things differently to the 'norm' and will help you feel more comfortable and empowered in doing so

Here are some suggestions of how you can explain PDA to others:

- 'X has a type of autism known as PDA. This means that they have very high anxiety and find everyday demands very difficult.'
- 'X is autistic and finds the demands of Christmas Day very hard. We are having a quiet Christmas Day at home, you are welcome to join us but X may not be able to come out of their room and join us.'

If you get invited to a family event or party you don't have to stay for the whole thing, you can go for the first or last part. You may also find it helpful to identify a safe space for your child to access if their anxiety gets too high. You can also just say 'No thank you' to invitations if you feel that this is what is best for you and your child, or limit the amount of time people stay, without attributing the reasons for this to your child. Remember to do what works best for you and your family. If you are reading this as a family member, please understand that Christmas and other celebrations may look different to what you are used to or expecting.

Another thing that I recommend to families is 'Divide and Conquer', but what we are conquering here is the expectation that you have to do everything as a family unit. If your expectation is that you are all going to go out as a family and have a wonderful day together, where everyone gets on and no one gets dysregulated, it is likely you will be disappointed.

I worked with a lovely family years ago who had three children, the eldest of whom was PDA. My client told me that she looked forward to family time at the weekends where they would spend time together, often away from the home going to parks, museums or other attractions. It always ended badly. Eventually I suggested to my client that she should stop the expectation of having a 'nice day together' and that she and her husband take one or two children each and do something separately. This was far more successful in terms of keeping everyone calm and regulated. Like this family, it may work far better for your PDAer to spend time with just one parent, away from siblings, whilst another parent or family member takes other children out. You can then come back together later in the day when, hopefully, everyone has had a good day and spend some short but sweet quality time together. If you are a grandparent, family member or friend it may really help parents of a PDAer if you offer to take them or a sibling for a day to give everyone some undivided attention or a bit of a break.

## The power of yet

Finally, I would also like to remind you of 'The Power of Yet'. There are likely lots of things that your child or your family cannot do...

yet. Nothing is permanent and things do change. Adding 'yet' on to statements about what you or your child cannot do at the moment will help remind you of this and help you feel more positive about how things may look in the future.

It can of course be scary stepping off the well-trodden path that you thought parenting would be. It may feel like you are initially stumbling along blindly, but let your instincts and your child with PDA lead you, and eventually the new path you create will feel safer, more comfortable, calmer and much happier than the original route you were on.

## Chapter 5

# Supporting the Family and Yourself

This chapter is mostly aimed at parents and carers. It will be helpful also for wider family members and friends, and professionals such as social workers, education welfare officers or home school link workers to read.

Most people, before becoming parents, have an image in their minds of what parenting will look like, but as we have already discussed in the previous chapter, raising a child with PDA means doing things differently and going against the grain. Whenever we go against the grain, it always feels rough and uncomfortable initially. There will be some splinters. But when you continue to go against the grain, it starts to feel easier and easier, and eventually it will feel natural and smooth.

Unfortunately, when you parent differently, you won't always experience support from everyone in your life and not everyone will get it. You may receive unhelpful comments, judgement or even criticism from others, and this can be hard to deal with, especially if they are received from family or close friends.

They say it takes a village to raise a child, and that may well be true; but if all the villagers don't have a map of the village, then they won't be able to navigate it properly. One of our roles as parents is to sometimes give people a new version of the map, but also to realise that not everyone will be prepared to read and use it.

Sadly, many parents I know who have children with additional needs have had to distance themselves from family members or friends who don't get it. This is particularly the case with PDA families. First, because PDA parenting looks so different to 'traditional' parenting, and second, because children with PDA are such proficient maskers that other family members or professionals simply do not see the behaviour that parents see at home. This can mean

that parents get blamed for their child's behaviour because 'they don't behave that way when they are here'.

I also know so many parents of PDAers who have been on the receiving end of incredibly unhelpful comments like:

- 'You are way too soft!'
- 'You are letting them get away with it.'
- 'I wouldn't let them speak to me like that.'
- 'They are fine when they are with me!'

Comments like this show a complete misunderstanding of PDA but can also start to erode your confidence as a parent too. You may start to question yourself and the new path you have taken – but remember that your new approach is what is best for you and your child.

If you live with a spouse or partner, you are not always going to agree on every approach with your PDA child. That is OK, but it is really important that your child does not see or hear you disagreeing or discussing them negatively. Remember how sensitive your PDAer is to the environment – and that includes being sensitive to you. Tense conversations through gritted teeth could be overheard by a PDAer who may then blame themselves for the conflict or try to play one parent off against the other. If you find yourself disagreeing with the way your spouse or partner is parenting, then either find a way to calmly interject or agree a quiet time away from your child to discuss it later. Sometimes the only way to move forward is to agree to disagree.

When extended family or friends offer you 'helpful' comments, it may be a good idea to be prepared with some helpful yet assertive comments of your own. These templates may be useful:

**Fact**: 'Billy has PDA which means he will find the demand of sitting at the table with us very difficult.'

**Sympathy**: 'I know you like it when the family sit together.'

**Solution**: 'He can eat his meal in his bedroom then come and join us if he feels comfortable later.'

or

**Fact**: 'Daisy's PDA means that she finds speaking really hard sometimes.'

**Sympathy**: 'I know manners are important to you.'

**Solution**: 'Daisy will find other ways to let us know she is grateful.'

It will also be helpful to explain to siblings and other young members of the family, such as cousins, about your child's PDA so that they understand the reasons that you are treating your PDAer differently at times. (Eliza and I have written *The Kid's Simple Guide to PDA* for this very purpose.)

## Looking after yourself

There is no doubt about it that parenting a child with PDA is going to be hard work at times. If you are parenting a PDAer, you are parenting an autistic child with a strong sense of autonomy who believes that they are equal to you and who cannot tolerate what appear to be 'simple demands'. You are probably also having to defend your parenting at times, and if your child is school age then you are likely to be fighting for the right provision for them too. You would not be human if this did not get to you at times.

It is so important to protect your mental health, primarily for your own sake, but also for the sake of your PDAer too. There is a saying, 'You are only as happy as your least happy child.' PDAers are so sensitive to other people's feelings and emotions that the expression 'You are only as regulated as the least regulated person near you' would probably apply to most PDAers most of the time.

Your own emotional regulation can really impact on your PDAer. I once worked with a young person who told me that their dad was 'always angry' with them, and as a result they were arguing most evenings after he returned from work. When I spoke with the family, it transpired that the young person's dad was having a really stressful time at work and was walking into the home every night stressed out, not angry. This was misconstrued by the PDAer, who would confront their dad every night by asking him what they had done wrong – which then resulted in conflict. It really helped the dad to understand how confused his son was by the message he was receiving, and it helped the young person to understand that his dad's stress was not related to him.

I am not saying for a moment that you should hide your true emotions around PDAers. This is actually the last thing I would suggest, as PDAers will sniff out anything that is fake anyway. I think it can actually be incredibly helpful to be completely honest about your feelings, and then you can role-model that it is OK to feel these emotions and what you can do to support yourself when you have them.

For example, you could say: 'I have had a really difficult day at work today and I am feeling really stressed. Before I have dinner, I am going to go outside into the garden and take some big deep breaths,' or 'It is making me feel really angry that no one is listening to me today. I don't want to shout at anyone, so I am going to go upstairs and listen to a podcast for a bit until I feel calmer.'

To protect your own mental health, it is important that you take time out when you can. Even if this is just for a few minutes each day to go for a walk, listen to some music or an audiobook or take a hot bath. The stronger your own mental health is, the stronger you can be for your child.

Don't be scared to ask for help when you need it, but seek help from the right people. Find and speak to people who understand and avoid those who don't. There are some really helpful groups on social media, but some of them, in my opinion, paint a very negative and therefore unhelpful picture of PDA. The right support is vital, and you need to find your radiators (those people who make you feel stronger) and remove the drains (those who don't) from your life. As I have mentioned above, if you are a family member or friend, then offers of support in the form of childcare, picking up shopping or doing some laundry, etc., may be gratefully received.

Remember there is no such thing as a 'normal family', and that comparing yourself with others, and what you thought your parenting journey was going to look like, is rarely going to bring you much happiness because, as one of my favourite sayings goes, 'Comparison is the thief of joy.'

Comparison

IS THE

THIEF OF

JOY

Parenting a child with PDA is going to take you on routes you didn't even know existed! It may not be the journey you were expecting to go on, but I can promise you that, although it will be a bumpy ride at times, your passenger will be great company, funny, determined and adventurous (and probably fairly bossy!). If you trust them to show you the way, you will get to the destination together and have loads of fun in the process!

Chapter 6

# Supporting the Individual and Family in Times of Crisis

This chapter will be helpful for parents, carers, wider
family members and friends, and professionals
such as social workers, SENCOs, education welfare
officers or home school link workers to read.

There will be times when your PDAer's bucket fills up, and this could
be completely out of your control. If they are in school, they may
come home with a full bucket, or their bucket could be filling up
due to the many micro demands that they are having to manage
every single minute of every day.

Once the bucket is full, it is important to remember that there
is no capacity left for any further demands. This could explain why
your child cannot eat or speak when they get home from school

and will need a vital period of low- or no-demand time to allow them to recover.

It is also important to remember that when the bucket is full and your child's anxiety levels are very high, their cognitive ability will be significantly impaired. Their ability to think and process will be far less than normal, so even asking a question such as 'What's the matter?' or 'Why did you do that?' is likely to cause further distress.

Asking your child to get changed, do their homework or even answer questions about their school day when their bucket is at capacity is likely to result in a meltdown or shutdown response. When the bucket is full the individual's brain is focused only on survival, and this means that your PDAer is likely to have one of the following responses:

- Fight (becoming physically or verbally aggressive).
- Flight (running away).
- Freeze (being unable to speak or move).
- Fawn (trying to please the person who is causing the threat).

Other responses to anxiety are Flopping (jelly legs) or Flocking (finding safety in numbers).

Your PDAer may react differently on different days, but it is vital to remember that their response to anxiety is not a choice but a reflex reaction to the threat that they are under. Although it can be extremely challenging to support someone when they are experiencing one of the above reactions, we have to remember that *they are having a hard time, not giving you a hard time.*

Most of the children and young people I work with will tell me that when they feel anxious they need two things, and those two things are Time and Space.

Your child is unlikely to verbalise to you calmly that they need these things. Not all children will externalise their anxiety and many PDAers will internalise it and have a 'shutdown' where they may only be able to communicate their need for time and space by becoming mute, zoning out and not speaking at all.

If your child externalises their anxiety, they may start screaming at you to 'Fuck off!' or tell you that they hate you or may make very personal comments that they know will hurt your feelings. They may throw things or spit at you or deliberately break things that they know are precious to you. These things are all communicating that they need you to leave them alone. They want you to go because then you cannot place any further demands on them.

## Coping in moments of crisis

Even though your child may be communicating with you to leave them alone, your role as a parent when your child is in crisis is to keep them safe. This means that sometimes it will not be appropriate to leave them unattended. Sometimes you will need to stay with your child, but during this time you need to ensure that your communication both verbal and non-verbal is kept to a minimum.

One of the most important things you can do when your child is in crisis is to show them that you understand how they feel and validate their feelings.

Imagine that you were going for a job interview in a location you had never been to before. You really want this job and have been preparing for the interview for months. Your anxiety levels are almost certainly going to be raised as you set off for the interview, but now imagine that you get lost and cannot find the building where your interview is taking place. You look at your watch and realise that your interview starts very soon, and in a panic you call up and explain that you are lost and will be a few minutes late. The person on the other end of the phone says to you, 'That's really not acceptable, if you don't arrive for your interview on time you will forfeit your opportunity to apply for this position. We don't tolerate lateness here, and if you can't even make your interview on time you are not the right person for us.'

In this situation your anxiety levels are almost certainly going to go through the roof, and you will probably start to panic more. You may cry, shout or just give up and go home.

What you would need in this situation is validation, empathy and compassion. You would need the person on the other end of the phone to say something like 'Don't worry, sir/madam, the building can be pretty hard to find, and people are always getting lost. I am sure you must be feeling pretty stressed out, but I can let the panel know you are on your way, and we can push the interview back so you have plenty of time. I will make sure there is a drink of water ready for you when you arrive.'

I am sure you would still be anxious, but hopefully the response from the other end of the phone would calm you a little, rather than escalate you further.

When your child is anxious, saying things like 'I understand you are very angry right now,' or 'I can see that you are finding this incredibly hard,' or 'I know you hate it when X touches your stuff,' can be incredibly helpful to hear. You would need to ensure that your child is not so anxious that they cannot process this, which could escalate them further. Remember, sometimes silence is golden and just your calm and non-judgemental presence may be enough in that moment.

On the flipside, we need to avoid saying things that invalidate a person's feelings like:

- 'Calm down.'
- 'It's not that bad.'
- 'You will be OK.'
- 'You were fine last time.'
- 'You are overreacting.'

When an individual is in a state of high anxiety, the very last thing that they need to hear are threats, consequences or ultimatums such as:

- 'If you don't go to bed now you won't be able to go horse riding tomorrow.'
- 'If you don't stop shouting at me, I will have to take your Xbox away.'
- 'You can't have any ice-cream until you have eaten all your dinner.'

No one who is anxious will ever feel better when offered these things, and an ultimatum is the ultimate no-no for someone with PDA because they will feel that they have no autonomy or control at all!

Supporting someone who is in crisis is very stressful and can also be frightening. It is important to try to remain calm. Emotions can be contagious, particularly for PDAers who are so sensitive to other people's emotions. If your child is scared and shouting and you shout back, you are quickly going to enter into a conflict spiral which can be hard to break.

If you show your child that you are calm, they may see that the environment is safe, and this can help calm them down more quickly. This is known as co-regulation.

Co-regulation can occur when a safe, connected person can help regulate the emotions and behaviours of another person who is experiencing stress or anxiety. Co-regulation nurtures connections through strategies and calming techniques, so just sitting quietly with your child, breathing deeply, closing your eyes or listening

to music in the presence of your child can be incredibly helpful for them. Some children may respond well to humour or other distractions.

If you don't feel that you can stay calm and you feel that you are in danger of becoming escalated and shouting, often the best thing to do is remove yourself from the situation if you can.

It may be that when you leave your child's space, they calm down more quickly because you are reducing the demand of them having to communicate with you, but obviously you should only leave your child if it is safe to do so.

If you are reading this book as an extended family member, it may be that the best support you can provide is to the parents themselves: checking in with them afterwards; letting them express their feelings without judgement; or even providing some practical support, such as an offer to pick up groceries and basically taking smaller jobs off their hands to help at a point when they may be feeling quite overwhelmed.

## Recovering from crisis

After someone has been in crisis, shutdown or meltdown, there will need to be a period of recovery and healing, and the nervous system will need a chance to re-set itself. You also need to give your child time for their adrenaline levels to go back to baseline levels so that they are not triggered back into crisis again.

A good way to think about this is to imagine a kettle that you boil first thing in the morning when you wake up. When you boil the kettle for the first time it will probably take about two minutes to go from room temperature to boiling; however, the water in the kettle will stay really hot for ages and will probably take about an hour to go back to room temperature again.

Like the kettle, it will take the person a considerable amount of time to 'cool down' – in fact, it can take at least 45 minutes for adrenaline levels to go to back to baseline levels after a crisis.

If you press the 'on' button on a kettle that has recently boiled, it will boil much more quickly as the water is still warm. Similarly, if a person who has recently been in a state of high anxiety is triggered whilst their adrenaline levels are still raised, they are likely to hit crisis again very quickly.

After your child has been in crisis, they may hit a very emotional low. They may feel embarrassed, guilty or ashamed about the way they have acted. I have heard of children with PDA saying things like 'I am a terrible person' or 'I don't deserve to be alive' after they have been in crisis. These things are obviously very hard to hear, but it is so important that we do not compound these feelings with our own reactions. After a crisis your child will need reassurance that you still love them and that you can keep them safe.

It is important to wait until everyone is calm before you talk about what happened. Remember that your child could find a discussion about a situation very demanding, particularly if they are feeling embarrassed or ashamed.

Your child may not want to talk about what has happened, and they may not be able to fully recall their actions before or during the crisis because of the changes that occur in the brain at these points. I would not waste your time asking your child 'Why did you do that?!' because you probably won't get the answer you were hoping for. Your child may not know why they did something. They may know but not want to tell you. They may know but not know how to tell you.

Instead of asking 'Why did you do that?!' it may be better to say something like 'That was clearly very difficult for you. Is there anything I can do to help you next time?' or 'That didn't go too well did it? What could we do differently next time together?'

It is important to look for patterns in your child's behaviour, and it may be helpful to keep a diary. If you notice that Sunday nights are always very difficult for your child, perhaps their anxiety is building because they have school the next day. Or perhaps anxiety is worse on a Wednesday morning because they have football practice later that day. Looking for clues will help you to focus on the underlying causes of anxiety, which can then be addressed, rather than dealing with the anxiety itself.

I would also like to remind you that it is OK to 'lose your shit' sometimes! You are a human being, and at times your children are going to push you to the point where your own bucket fills up.

It can be very powerful for your child to hear that you made a mistake in the way that you dealt with a situation, and that you can apologise for this. Saying 'I am sorry I shouted at you. I felt really angry when you broke my picture, and I did not react well. Next time I will try and take some deep breaths before I speak so that I do not shout at you,' can be a very positive message for your child to hear.

Here again you are role-modelling that there is nothing wrong with having big emotions, but that it is what we do with those emotions that is important. Apologising to a child is also extremely important as it lets them know that we all make mistakes sometimes and shows your PDA child that you have an equal relationship, which is important to them.

You may find that it is easier for you to have post-crisis conversations with your child in less confrontational situations, such as in the car, on a walk or when they are in the bath. They may also prefer to communicate with you by using their phone to send messages, GIFs or memes. The most important thing to remember is that your child will talk when they are ready, and you will not be able to force them into a conversation until they are.

## Keeping the rest of the family safe

If you have other children, then it is important to keep them safe when your PDAer is dysregulated. It is also important for them to understand that your child who is dysregulated is anxious and scared, and this is what is driving their behaviour.

You may find it helpful to use the bucket analogy with all your children and explain that, when your PDA child's bucket is full, they may have a fight response and they are not choosing to act this way.

You could use an analogy that we have used in our other book, *The Kid's Simple Guide to PDA*, to help your other children understand an anxiety-based response:

Imagine you go to a friend's house, and they explain that they have just rescued a new puppy. They tell you that the dog is very nervous and scared, and when you go to stroke the dog it growls at you and backs away.

Although you may feel upset and a little frightened that the puppy has growled at you, it is important to understand that the puppy is not being 'bad' or 'naughty'. The puppy growled because it is scared and anxious.

Hopefully, you would also understand that if you shouted at the puppy, or smacked it, it would get even more frightened. And if you did this again, the puppy would growl again and may even bite you. The situation would be likely to get much, much worse.

The best way to get the puppy to feel safe is to be very calm around it or to give it lots of time and space to feel safe and to trust you. Eventually, if you give the puppy lots of space and are very calm and gentle, the puppy may start to trust you and be able to come closer. The calmer and gentler you are with the puppy, the safer it will feel to be around you.

It may be helpful for you to discuss a safety plan with your other children for when your PDA child becomes very dysregulated. You could agree that they go to their room, into the garden or, if they are old enough, out for a walk until you can reassure them that things are calm again. It will be important that all family members or friends visiting the house are aware of these plans that have been put in place so that they can also support accordingly when needed.

It will also be helpful for you to talk to them about not retaliating or reacting to physical or verbal behaviours, whilst acknowledging how hard this can be at times. It is key to show your other children that you empathise and understand how difficult it can be for them sometimes. Using the Fact, Sympathy, Solution technique may be helpful here. For example:

**Fact**: 'When Alex's bucket gets full, he finds it really hard to control his behaviours.'

**Sympathy**: 'I know you hate it when he acts like this, I find it really hard too.'

**Solution**: 'Stay in your room until he is calm and then we can talk about it together.'

You may also need to reassure your children that you are not treating them differently because you love them less, but because of their individual and different needs.

It may feel that the times when siblings get on is limited, but do make a point of 'catching your children being good'; and when they are getting on find a positive consequence linked to this, such as 'Thank you for playing nicely together, it meant I was able to get my work finished, so you can spend some more time on the Xbox now whilst I get on with dinner.'

Although it is undoubtedly very challenging to manage a child who is having regular meltdowns or shutdowns, do remember that this time will pass, particularly if you can identify and reduce the anxiety, demands and triggers that are filling up their bucket. Meeting your child's anxiety with love, compassion and validation, reducing demands and remembering that tomorrow is a new day will help you all move forward more positively.

At the end of this book there are some useful links for parents who are supporting children who display aggressive behaviour.

Chapter 7

# PDA and Education

This chapter will be helpful for parents, carers, wider family members and friends, and professionals such as education staff, SENCOs, social workers, education welfare officers or home school link workers to read.

There is absolutely no denying that school can be an incredibly challenging environment for children and young people with PDA. In 2018 The PDA Society conducted a study entitled *Being Misunderstood* (see 'Resources' section at the end of the book). The results of the study showed that of the 969 children and young people with a PDA profile surveyed, 70 per cent of them were not able to tolerate a school environment.

Hopefully you now have a good understanding of why school or college is so difficult for PDAers, but, in short, learning environments are incredibly demanding places.

Just getting into school each morning requires a child to be able to meet dozens of demands, and then once they are there the demands of learning, socialising, communicating, transitioning, 'behaving' and managing the sensory environment will just keep on coming relentlessly.

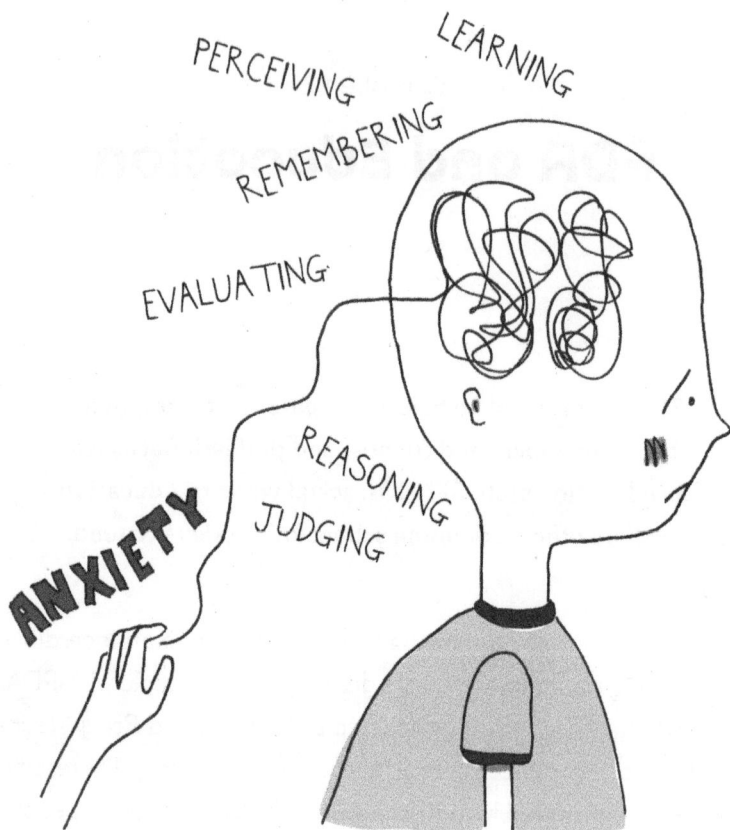

A pattern I see very regularly with children I work with in the UK is that some are able to manage in the primary system but find the transition into secondary school incredibly challenging or just impossible. Primary schools are usually more nurturing and are much smaller with fewer transitions. The secondary system is more demanding for our children as secondary schools are so much bigger and have more transitions and less autonomy around learning.

When looking for a school for your child with PDA, there is one very important thing you should listen to – your gut! Go and visit as many schools as you can, and if your gut tells you it is not right for your child then it isn't.

I do have to stress that during my time working as an education consultant I have worked with some amazing schools that really do get it. If 70 per cent of children with PDA are not in school, then 30 per cent are. There are definitely some fantastic schools out there that are doing a great job.

I am often asked 'What is the best type of school for a child with PDA?' and the answer to that is that there is not a type. I have worked with amazing mainstream schools, brilliant specialist schools and some independent schools too.

So, what made these schools so amazing? They all have a few *key* elements in common:

- a highly supportive head teacher and senior leadership team who not only understand PDA but support all their staff in promoting PDA-friendly approaches
- an understanding of the autonomy and need for freedom that PDAers have
- an understanding of the difference between 'I can't' and 'I won't'
- an understanding of anxiety, its many different guises and the essential individual support strategies required for children with this profile
- an understanding that children with PDA cannot be 'made' to do anything
- a commitment to staff training
- a commitment to supporting staff when things are not going well
- a fantastic working relationship with parents and full and transparent communication
- an understanding that there will be good days and bad days, and that progress with a PDA child will never be linear
- an ability to weave the child's frequently changing interests into the curriculum
- an ability to pick their battles!
- an understanding that the most important thing for a child with PDA is that they feel *safe* with the people they are with and the environment they are in
- a flexible, spontaneous and child-led approach.

You will note that all of the above don't actually cost any money and are more about the ethos and spirit of the school and, most importantly, the people who work in it.

In the UK, schools have a legal obligation under the Equality Act of 2010 to make reasonable adjustments for any child or young person with additional needs. *Your child does need to have a diagnosis for reasonable adjustments to be made* and some of the best schools I have worked with have made excellent reasonable adjustments based on need for a child not diagnosed with a PDA profile. Reasonable adjustments ensure that a child is not at any disadvantage because of their needs compared to their peers.

Some examples of reasonable adjustments for a child with PDA may include:

- a safe person and a safe place that can be accessed during times of high anxiety in the day
- tasks broken down into smaller chunks to help with understanding and processing
- a Time Out or Exit card or system (sometimes the use of a card creates a demand so just being able to leave a classroom without permission to access an agreed safe space can significantly reduce anxiety)
- alternatives to writing, such as a scribe or use of technology
- regular movement breaks when needed and the use of fiddle toys
- considering the environment from the child's unique sensory perspective – for example, not sitting a child near busy displays, closing windows to avoid outside noise, understanding that they don't like the texture of certain materials like

paper or glue, letting them get ready for PE in the classroom instead of a noisy (and possibly smelly) changing room

- a reduced or flexible timetable – for example, not having to attend PE lessons if this is a source of anxiety
- a soft start to the day – for example, going to the library to read or listen to music rather than straight in to the demanding classroom
- a check-out at the end of the day to discuss any concerns or successes that have occurred that day
- alternative activities or locations for playtime and lunchtime
- not having to complete homework or being offered time in school to complete homework.

Sometimes reasonable adjustments are not enough, and in the UK many children with a PDA profile will have an Education Health Care Plan (EHCP) to ensure that their needs are being met, especially where additional funding is required. The US equivalent is the Individualized Education Program (IEP). Securing an EHCP for your child is not an easy task, and it may be helpful for you to seek some advice and support to get one. There are many services available to help take you through the lengthy process of getting an EHCP, including advocates and solicitors, but again do your homework as it can be a bit like the Wild West out there.

You can ask your child's school to apply for an EHCP for you, or you can do a parental application.

Another very helpful resource available on The PDA Society website is an example of an EHCP written for a child with a PDA profile, which you can adapt for your own child.

If your child is in school, then building a good rapport with the school SENCO (UK) or Special Education Administrator (USA) will be essential to ensure there is good communication regarding your child at all times. A good school will work *with* you and will recognise that whilst they are the experts in education, you are the expert in your child.

As I say in *The Educator's Experience of Pathological Demand Avoidance*:

> Regular meetings and good communication are essential when supporting a learner with PDA. During these meetings everyone's voices and opinions are listened to with equal importance and validity. Where I have seen the most success is where everyone works together with the child's needs at the heart of everything.

(If you are an educator reading this book, you might like to pick up a copy of *The Educator's Experience of Pathological Demand Avoidance* for more advice and guidance.)

Even if your child manages to get to school and stay for the day, they are probably coming home with a bucket that is at capacity. As I have mentioned in previous chapters, it is vital that when your child returns from school or college they are given a period of low- or no-demand time so that they can let their bucket evaporate. Even asking your child 'Did you have a good day at school?' or suggesting that they get changed will create further anxiety and could cause shutdown or meltdown. Your child may just need time on their own in their room online or listening to music before they can cope with any further demands that day.

There may come a time when you realise that the school your child is in just isn't working, despite reasonable adjustments being made and a robust EHCP being in place. Your gut may be telling you that your child needs to be a part of the 70 per cent who cannot attend school.

Although this may be a very difficult decision to make, I can honestly say I do not know a single parent who has regretted the decision to de-register their child from school to either home educate them or, in the UK, secure an EOTAS/EOTIS (Education Other Than At/In School) package for their child.

An EOTAS package is funded by your local authority and will pay for specialist tutors and therapists to work with your child, most often within their home. Your child will need an EHCP to get EOTAS and you will have to be able to evidence that your child's needs cannot be met by any other school or provision. It can be extremely difficult to secure an EOTAS package, and it is likely that you will need evidence from other professionals such as an educational psychologist, which can be expensive too.

Now, I have to be honest and confess to being very biased here, but I am a *huge* fan of EOTAS for individuals with a PDA profile. I have seen children and young people with PDA whose lives and mental health have been utterly transformed with EOTAS.

EOTAS works for PDAers because children are supported according to their own unique strengths and needs. EOTAS works because it is:

**Equitable**: EOTAS programmes must be one of the most equitable types of education that exist. Children are supported according to their own unique strengths and needs. EOTAS programmes recognise that not all children are able to do the same thing at the same time and allow children to work at their own pace. Children can make rapid progress, without boundaries, and can slow down, pause or change direction when needed.

**Original**: Every EOTAS programme is unique, original and tailor-made to the learner's needs. No two programmes are the same, and programmes can be adapted and changed as children's interests and passions change.

**Transformative**: I hear this word so much from parents who have children who have EOTAS. EOTAS can literally transform children's mental health, their feelings about education and their future opportunities. The impact of EOTAS can send positive ripples through entire families. Children who have previously been described as 'defiant', 'oppositional' and 'challenging' become engaged, interested and excited by learning.

**Autonomous**: EOTAS allows true autonomy. Learners are the absolute *heart* of their programmes. *They* are in charge of what they want to learn about and when. EOTAS programmes can adapt and change as learners' interests change. Children learn because they want to, how they want to, about the things that they see the value of.

**Safe**: Learners who have EOTAS form safe, trusting, reciprocal connections with adults who can share their interests and passions. For children who have had such negative, traumatic experiences in education, this can take time, but EOTAS allows them the time they need, and the safe connections that are formed are the most important foundation of their education.

I just wish so much, that EOTAS was not regarded as 'less than' education in a school, and I wish that it was not so hard for children to get. I truly hope that one day it will be so much easier for children to be awarded this type of alternative education along with a greater understanding of the fact that school is not the right environment for many children and young people and that there are alternatives that should be held in equal regard to traditional schooling.

Whether you decide to fight for EOTAS or decide to home educate your child, there are a few important things to consider before you start:

- Your child may need a period of recovery after they are de-registered from school, particularly if they are experiencing burnout – this is known as 'unschooling'. For some children, school experiences will have been very negative and highly traumatic, and they need time to process and adjust.
- Allow plenty of time to build up trust with new people that they may meet, and build up new connections gradually to avoid overwhelm.
- Unschooling is an important process for parents to go through too. If you find yourself suddenly home educating or managing an EOTAS package, there may be a grieving period or an adjustment period as you and your child get used to a new way of life. Take your time and give yourself a chance to adjust and prepare for a new way of living.
- Don't try to recreate a school within your home. That environment did not work for your child, so don't try to turn your home into a school. You don't even need to follow a typical school day starting at 9.00 and finishing at 3.00; you can work flexibly, when your child is at their most creative and energetic.
- Reach out and make connections with other children and families who are not traditionally educating their children. You will feel less isolated, and it may also give your child the opportunity to make friends if they want to.

Finally, if you do decide to pursue EOTAS or home education, it does not have to be for ever. I know many children and young people who have transitioned back into school, college and even university after a period of time away from traditional education. Learning is a journey, and the destination can be reached by many routes. Alternatives to traditional education can simply be a detour rather than a complete change of direction, but your child will probably get to their destination far happier and healthier.

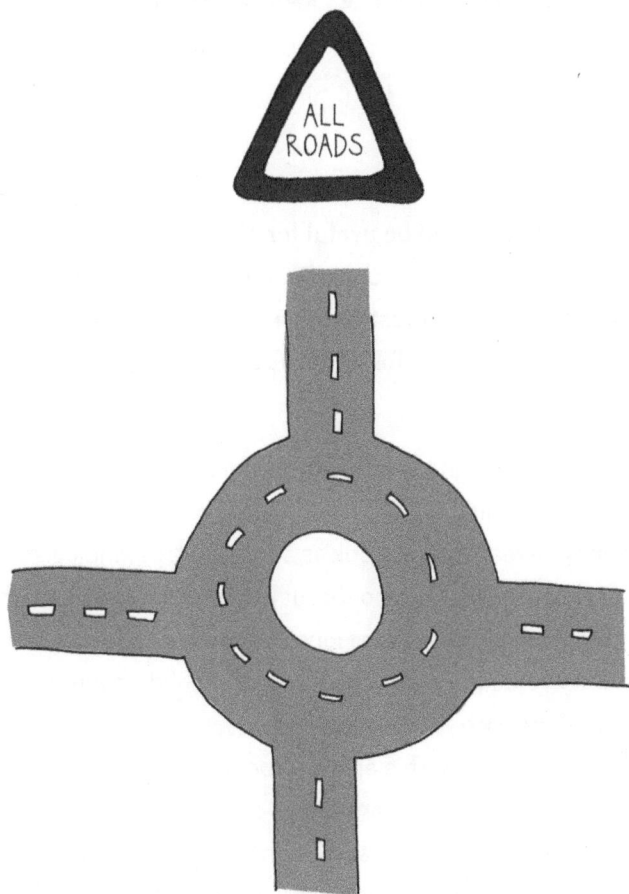

## Chapter 8

# Preparing to Work with PDAers

This chapter will be useful for all professionals to read, and also parents and carers to help them ask for reasonable adjustments and accommodations before professional appointments.

If you are lucky enough to work with PDAers, I hope you now have a better understanding of PDA having read some or all of this book.

You may be reading this book as a therapist, psychologist, tutor or peripatetic teacher, Guide or Scout leader or sports coach who is starting to work with a PDAer. Hopefully you will have the time and opportunity to build up a rapport with the child or young person you are working with.

You may be reading this as a doctor, nurse, dentist or medical professional who will have limited or one-off interactions with a PDAer. This means that it may be harder for you to build up trust and rapport with a PDAer before they meet with you.

To make appointments as easy as possible for a PDAer, try to provide succinct information beforehand about what they may expect in the appointment. It may help to send photos of yourself and the environment before they come, or allow them to visit the environment or have a practice run before they attend their appointment. Be clear about what the PDAer can expect to happen in the appointment.

Allow them to bring things to show you as part of the appointment or session with you. Ask questions and show genuine interest in their interests, as this will really help build rapport. If possible, allow extra time in appointments to build this.

Ensure that the PDAer has an exit route and can take a break if they need it. Could you agree a code word or signal if they need a break?

If possible, allow extra time for appointments so no one feels rushed or under pressure. Work with parents to find the best time of day for appointments (e.g. first thing in the morning to prevent anxiety building or last thing in the day to allow extra time to prepare).

Remember, the better connection you build with a PDAer, the safer they will feel.

Here are some key facts and essentials about PDA:

- PDA is a profile of autism that is characterised by high anxiety and a need for autonomy.
- Individuals with PDA are autistic and will experience difficulties with social communication. They will also have sensory differences and challenges.
- For an individual with PDA, demands are a threat to their autonomy and will trigger an anxiety-based reaction.
- Remember that *anxiety* is what drives the behaviour of an

individual with PDA. If you always consider the anxiety rather than the behaviour you are more likely to look for solutions and try to help. Also remember that sometimes anxiety stops individuals with PDA doing the things they want to do as well as the things they don't.

- PDAers don't always see hierarchy and status and may consider themselves as equal to adults. This means that they may feel patronised if you speak to them like a child, so speak to them and treat them as equals.

- Do not speak over the child or speak about the child to their parents in their hearing.

- A PDAer may be very blunt and honest in their communication. This does not mean that they are being rude, and they should not be reprimanded for their honesty. You cannot expect a neurodivergent child to behave like a neurotypical child or have neurotypical responses.

- Don't take offence if the PDAer does not speak or engage with you. This again is not down to rudeness but will indicate a high level of anxiety and lack of trust.

- Be aware of your non-verbal language. Individuals with PDA can be hypersensitive to tone of voice, facial expressions and body language, which can often cause them increased anxiety as they may misinterpret what you mean, feel easily patronised or pick up on the very subtle clues you are giving about the way you are feeling.

- Use a flexible, non-directive approach. Use phrases such as 'I wonder how we might...', 'I wonder if this will work if we do it like this...'.

- Offer choices. This gives the individual greater autonomy and can help to lower anxiety and help them feel that they have some control. Examples include 'Would you like to do X or Y first?' and 'Would you like to sit here or here?'

- Use challenges, games and races. 'I bet you can't finish before me!' Make sure you are joining in these genuinely so that the result becomes a shared goal.

- Praise can be difficult for PDAers to hear and accept, so praise indirectly. Let them hear you talking about them in a positive way or use 'I' statements, such as 'I don't think I know how to do that, so I am impressed that you do!'

- Reduce pressures and pick your battles. There will be days when anxiety is too high for an individual to cope with any demands. Ask yourself 'Does it really matter?' and if the answer is no, then pull back and reduce the demand.

- Have a sense of humour! Be prepared to take the mickey out of yourself and make appointments as fun and engaging as possible.

- Talk about areas of specific interest that the PDAer has, ask questions and show genuine interest.

- Depersonalise rules. 'I am afraid you can't go outside as it's slippery and our health and safety rules forbid it,' or 'It's the law, but I know it is really annoying!' Use facts not opinions.

- Show empathy and validate their anxiety. 'I know you hate coming to have your teeth checked. I used to hate it too when I was younger.'

- Understand that the individual with PDA may be masking – you may not see how much they are struggling and may see a very different presentation to the one parents are describing.

- Have fun! Enjoy your time with your PDA client and make sure you learn as much from them as they do from you.

# Final thoughts

There is no doubt about it, parenting or working with an individual with PDA will sometimes be challenging. At times you will question yourself, and others may question you too. You will need to establish new ways of doing things that will initially feel alien and strange, but the more you do things 'The PDA Way' the more natural they will feel and the more comfortable you will feel too.

The PDAer in your life needs safe, equal, authentic, genuine connections with others that they know are on their side. You need to work together as equal partners, following each other's lead and being there to catch them, without judgement, when needed. It may not always be an easy ride, and the balance may sometimes be hard to find, but I promise you it will be the most rewarding one you will ever take, and the final destination will 100 per cent be worth it.

# Resources

**PDA Society publications**
*Being Misunderstood: Experiences of the Pathological Demand Avoidance Profile of ASD.* Available at www.pdasociety.org.uk/wp-content/uploads/2019/08/BeingMisunderstood.pdf

*Education, Health and Care Plans to Support a PDA Profile of Autism.* Available at www.pdasociety.org.uk/wp-content/uploads/2021/07/EHCP-guide-FINAL-2.1.pdf

**Advice and guidance for educators**
Kerbey, L. (2023) *The Educator's Experience of Pathological Demand Avoidance.* London: Jessica Kingsley Publishers.

**Dealing with aggressive behaviour**
www.newboldhope.org
https://capafirstresponse.org

**Teaching social and emotional concepts**
www.5pointscale.com